My United States
Nevada

D1198564

JOSH GREGORY

Children's Press®
An Imprint of Scholastic Inc.

Content Consultant
James Wolfinger, PhD, Associate Dean and Professor
College of Education, DePaul University, Chicago, Illinois

Library of Congress Cataloging-in-Publication Data
Names: Gregory, Josh, author.
Title: Nevada / by Josh Gregory.
Description: New York, NY : Children's Press, an imprint of Scholastic Inc., [2018] | Series: A true book | Includes
  bibliographical references and index.
Identifiers: LCCN 2017025787 | ISBN 9780531231685 (library binding) | ISBN 9780531247198 (pbk.)
Subjects: LCSH: Nevada—Juvenile literature.
Classification: LCC F841.3 .G76 2018 | DDC 979.3—dc23
LC record available at https://lccn.loc.gov/2017025787

Photographs ©: cover: littleny/iStockphoto; back cover bottom: Prisma/Superstock, Inc.; back cover ribbon:
AliceLiddelle/Getty ImagesGetty Images; 3 bottom: Visions of America, LLC/Alamy Images; 3 map: Jim McMahon; 4
left: James Hager/Media Bakery; 4 right: Alan Murphy/BIA/Minden Pictures; 5 top: Tim Fitzharris/Minden Pictures; 5
bottom: Catmando/Shutterstock; 7 center bottom: f11photo/iStockphoto; 7 bottom: tupungato/iStockphoto; 7 top:
robertcicchetti/iStockphoto; 7 center top: Arco Images GmbH/Alamy Images; 8-9: Tim Fitzharris/Minden Pictures; 11:
Larry Prosor/Superstock, Inc.; 12: Tim Fitzharris/Minden Pictures; 13: Craig Aurness/Corbis/VCG/Getty Images; 14:
Dennis Frates/Alamy Images; 15: Mark Newman/Getty Images; 16-17: myLoupe/Universal Images Group/Getty Images;
19: State of Nevada/Wikimedia; 20: Tigatelu/Dreamstime; 22 right: Stockbyte/Getty Images; 22 left: cbies/Shutterstock;
23 top left: Alan Murphy/BIA/Minden Pictures; 23 bottom right: James Hager/Media Bakery; 23 top right: Corbin17/
Alamy Images; 23 center: Catmando/Shutterstock; 23 bottom left: SeDmi/Shutterstock; 24-25: The Granger Collection;
27: Corbis Historical/Getty Images; 29: Universal History Archive/UIG/Getty Images; 30 bottom: Igor Vkv/Shutterstock;
30 top right: Petur Asgeirsson/Shutterstock; 30 top left: The Granger Collection; 31 top right: Steve Lewis Stock/Media
Bakery; 31 bottom right: Media Bakery; 31 top left: cbies/Shutterstock; 31 bottom left: f11photo/iStockphoto; 32: Ivan
Dmitri/Michael Ochs Archives/Getty Images; 33: Paul Fearn/Alamy Images; 34-35: Christian Heeb/AWL Images; 36:
Bill Stevenson/Media Bakery; 37: Darren Carroll /Sports Illustrated/Getty Images; 38: David Paul Morris/Bloomberg/
Getty Images; 39: Brooks Kraft LLC/Corbis/Getty Images; 40 inset: Dani Vincek/Shutterstock; 40 bottom: PepitoPhotos/
iStockphoto; 41: Andrew Peacock/Aurora Photos; 42 top: Bettmann/Getty Images; 42 bottom left: Aaron P. Bernstein/
Getty Images; 42 center right: Jennifer Lourie/WireImage/Getty Images; 42 bottom right: Jean Catuffe/GC Images/
Getty Images; 43 top left: Everett Collection Inc/Alamy Images; 43 top right: Rob Loud/WireImage/Getty Images; 43
bottom left: Steve Granitz/WireImage/Getty Images; 43 bottom center: C Flanigan/FilmMagic/Getty Images; 43 bottom
right: Gary Gershoff/WireImage/Getty Images; 44 bottom left: David Paul Morris/Bloomberg/Getty Images; 44 right:
Tim Fitzharris/Minden Pictures; 45 top: Joshua Resnick/Shutterstock; 45 center: iofoto/Shutterstock; 45 bottom: Craig
Aurness/Corbis/VCG/Getty Images.

Maps by Map Hero, Inc.

No part of this publication may be reproduced in whole or in part, or stored in a retrieval system, or transmitted
in any form or by any means, electronic, mechanical, photocopying, recording, or otherwise, without written
permission of the publisher. For information regarding permission, write to Scholastic Inc., Attention:
Permissions Department, 557 Broadway, New York, NY 10012.
© 2018 Scholastic Inc.

All rights reserved. Published in 2018 by Children's Press, an imprint of Scholastic Inc.
Printed in North Mankato, MN, USA 113

SCHOLASTIC, CHILDREN'S PRESS, A TRUE BOOK™, and associated logos are trademarks and/or registered
trademarks of Scholastic Inc.

Scholastic Inc., 557 Broadway, New York, NY 10012

1 2 3 4 5 6 7 8 9 10 R 27 26 25 24 23 22 21 20 19 18

Front cover: Las Vegas

Back cover: Great Basin National Park

Welcome to Nevada

Find the Truth!

Everything you are about to read is true **except** for one of the sentences on this page.

Which one is **TRUE**?

T or F   Nevada's name comes from the Spanish word for "desert."

T or F   Nevada became a U.S. state during the Civil War.

Find the answers in this book.

Key Facts

Capital: Carson City

Estimated population as of 2016: 2,940,058

Nicknames: Silver State, Sagebrush State

Biggest cities: Las Vegas, Henderson, Reno

UNITED STATES

← Nevada

Contents

Map: This Is Nevada! **6**

1 Land and Wildlife

What is the terrain of Nevada like
and what kinds of wildlife live there?. **9**

2 Government

What are the different parts
of Nevada's government? **17**

THE **BIG** TRUTH!

Mountain bluebird

What Represents Nevada?

Which designs, objects, plants,
and animals symbolize Nevada? **22**

Desert bighorn sheep

Valley of Fire State Park

3 History

How did Nevada become
the state it is today?

.... **25**

4 Culture

What do Nevadans do for work and fun?

.... **35**

Famous People **42**

Did You Know That **44**

Resources **46**

Important Words **47**

Index **48**

About the Author **48**

**Single-leaf pinyon
and bristlecone pine**

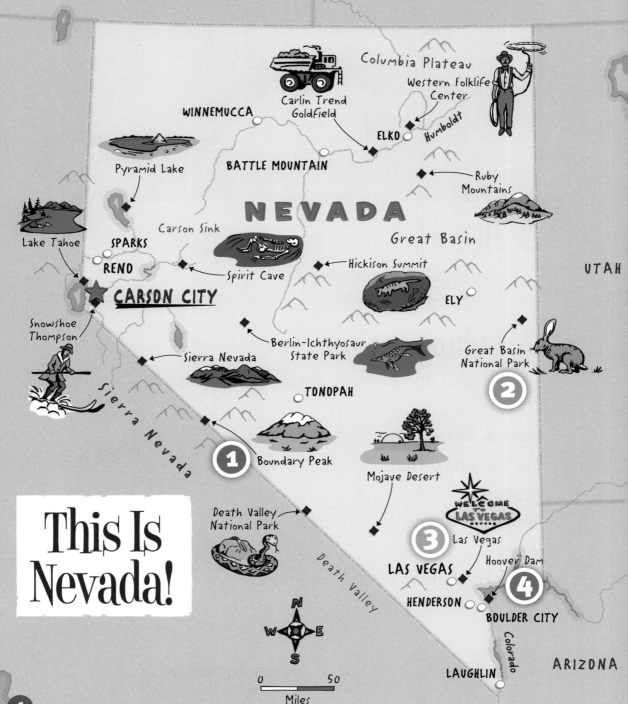

OREGON

IDAHO

Columbia Plateau

Carlin Trend
Goldfield

Western Folklife
Center

WINNEMUCCA

ELKO   Humboldt

Pyramid Lake

BATTLE MOUNTAIN

Ruby
Mountains

NEVADA

Carson Sink

Great Basin

Lake Tahoe

SPARKS

Spirit Cave

Hickison Summit

RENO

CARSON CITY

ELY

UTAH

Snowshoe
Thompson

Berlin-Ichthyosaur
State Park

Sierra Nevada

Great Basin
National Park

②

①

Boundary Peak

TONOPAH

Mojave Desert

Death Valley
National Park

WELCOME
TO
LAS VEGAS
NEVADA

③ Las Vegas

LAS VEGAS

Hoover Dam

④

Death Valley

HENDERSON

BOULDER CITY

Colorado

ARIZONA

This Is Nevada!

LAUGHLIN

N
W   E
S

0   50
Miles

6

❶ Boundary Peak

At 13,145 feet (4,007 meters) above sea level, this mountaintop is the highest point in Nevada. It attracts many climbers who want a view of Nevada's spectacular landscape.

❷ Great Basin National Park

This park offers a great opportunity to check out some of Nevada's most amazing natural wonders. The sights range from mountain forests to huge underground caves.

❸ Las Vegas Strip

Las Vegas is Nevada's biggest city and an international tourist destination. Check out the Las Vegas Strip, a part of the city known for its hotels and casinos. There are magic shows, live music, comedy, and much more!

❹ Hoover Dam

This enormous dam on the Colorado River forms Lake Mead and generates electricity for people in Nevada, Arizona, and California. You can visit to enjoy incredible views and tour the dam's interior.

More than two million people visit Red Rock Canyon National Conservation Area, located just outside Las Vegas, each year.

CHAPTER 1

Land and Wildlife

From the bright lights and bustling activity of the Las Vegas Strip to the dry, sandy expanse of the Mojave Desert, Nevada is a land of great contrasts. It's the seventh-largest state in the country, but the vast majority of its population lives in just a few areas. Huge parts of the state are largely empty of people. As remote as some areas are, however, they are worth visiting. There is plenty of natural beauty throughout Nevada.

Way Out West

Nevada's landscape consists mainly of deserts, mountains, and rocky canyons. There is also the occasional grassy valley. Several rivers and lakes are scattered across the state's rugged terrain. The longest river is the Humboldt River. It flows west across the northern part of the state for about 300 miles (483 kilometers), ending at an area in northwestern Nevada called the Humboldt Sink.

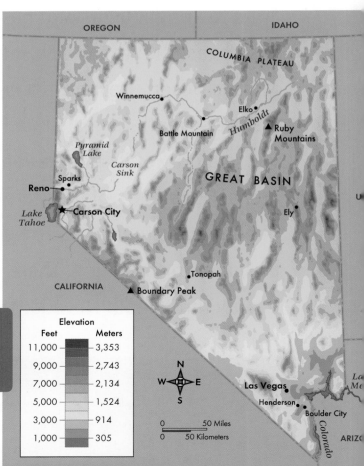

This map shows where the higher (orange and red) and lower (green) areas are in Nevada.

OREGON

IDAHO

COLUMBIA PLATEAU

Winnemucca

Elko

Humboldt

Battle Mountain

Ruby Mountains

Pyramid Lake

Carson Sink

GREAT BASIN

Sparks

Reno

Lake Tahoe

Carson City

Ely

Tonopah

CALIFORNIA

Boundary Peak

Elevation

Feet	Meters
11,000	3,353
9,000	2,743
7,000	2,134
5,000	1,524
3,000	914
1,000	305

N
W E
S

Las Vegas

Henderson

Boulder City

La Me

0   50 Miles
0   50 Kilometers

Colorado

ARIZ

Lake Tahoe

Located in the Sierra Nevada on Nevada's western border, Lake Tahoe is one of the largest lakes in the United States. Its shoreline runs a whopping 72 miles (116 km). Plunging to a depth of 1,645 feet (501 m), it is also among the country's deepest lakes. Unlike much of Nevada, Lake Tahoe is surrounded by lush, green forests. Nevadans love visiting the area to enjoy boating, hiking, and other activities. Skiing is also popular in the surrounding mountains during the winter.

Valley of Fire State Park is famous for its remarkable rock formations.

Most of Nevada lies within the Great Basin. This is the region between the Sierra Nevada in the west and Utah's Wasatch Mountains in the east. Between these mountain ranges, the land curves downward, forming a series of bowl-like shapes.

South of the Great Basin is the Mojave Desert. This region covers most of Nevada's southern tip and extends into the surrounding states. It is one of the hottest, driest parts of the country.

Climate

People in Nevada must be prepared for harsh weather. Winters in the north are long and very cold. Summers there are short and hot. Farther south, it is warm year-round, with extremely hot summers. One thing people across Nevada don't get much of is rain. Nevada is the driest state in the country. Much of its **precipitation** falls as snow high up in the mountains. **Drought** is common, and southern Nevada often goes weeks without rain.

MAXIMUM TEMPERATURE 125 °F

MINIMUM TEMPERATURE -50 °F

In the driest parts of Nevada, the ground can start to crack and split apart during long periods of drought.

Sagebrush plants do not need much water to survive.

Growing Up Tough

Most of Nevada's plants endure a harsh climate. Short, tough plants such as grasses, bushes, and cacti grow best in the state's deserts. Especially common are sagebrush plants, which give Nevada one of its nicknames: the Sagebrush State.

Up in the mountains, more trees grow. About 16 percent of the state is covered in mountainside forests. Firs, pines, junipers, and other evergreen species are found here.

Nevada's Creatures

Nevada's wild landscapes are home to a wide range of animal species. Large mammals such as bighorn sheep, mule deer, elk, and even wild horses roam the state's plains and valleys. Mountain goats climb rocky cliffs. Rattlesnakes, Gila monsters, and other reptiles are common in desert areas. So are small animals such as squirrels, rabbits, and kangaroo rats. Around lakes and rivers, many bird species thrive, including eagles, ducks, and pelicans.

Wild horses roam Nevada's Amargosa Desert.

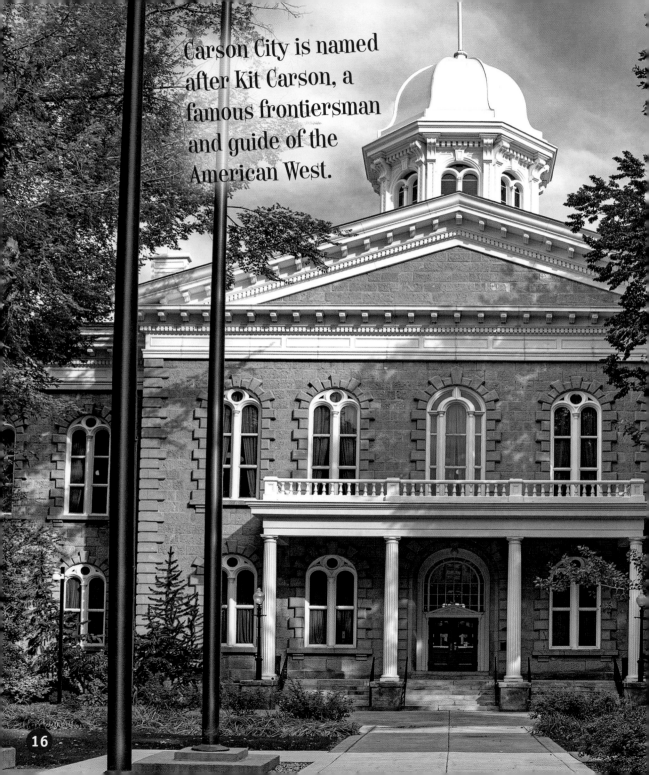

Carson City is named after Kit Carson, a famous frontiersman and guide of the American West.

Government

Carson City has served as Nevada's capital since the region became a U.S. **territory** in 1861. While it is far from the largest city in Nevada, Carson City is the center of activity for the state's government. Elected officials from all over the state gather here. They make important decisions about how to run the state, from debating new laws to determining how to use tax dollars.

The Three Branches

Nevada's government is divided into executive, legislative, and judicial branches. Each branch has different powers and responsibilities. This prevents any one of them from becoming more powerful than the others.

The executive branch oversees more than 200 departments and agencies. They deal with everything from education to law enforcement to transportation. The legislative branch creates new laws, while the judicial branch is the state's court system.

NEVADA'S STATE GOVERNMENT

LEGISLATIVE BRANCH
Writes and passes state laws

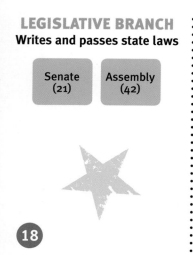

Senate (21) — Assembly (42)

EXECUTIVE BRANCH
Carries out state laws

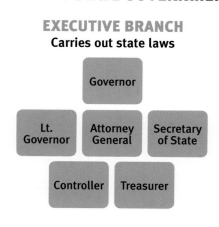

Governor

Lt. Governor — Attorney General — Secretary of State

Controller — Treasurer

JUDICIAL BRANCH
Enforces state laws

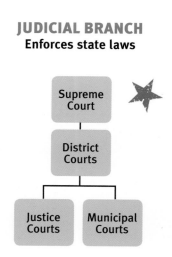

Supreme Court

District Courts

Justice Courts — Municipal Courts

A Blueprint for Government

On July 4, 1864, representatives from across Nevada met in Carson City. Their task was to begin creating the state's **constitution**. This document outlines the way the state government is organized, how taxes are collected, and more. Over the years, Nevada's constitution has been changed and updated with **amendments**. However, the original historical document continues to form the backbone of the state's government even today.

This handwritten page from 1864 records a telegraph message about Nevada's new state constitution that was sent to U.S. government officials in Washington, D.C.

Nevada in the National Government

Each state elects officials to represent it in the U.S. Congress. Like every state, Nevada has two senators. The U.S. House of Representatives relies on a state's population to determine its numbers. Nevada has four representatives in the House.

Every four years, states vote on the next U.S. president. Each state is granted a number of electoral votes based on its number of members in Congress. With two senators and four representatives, Nevada has six electoral votes.

2 senators and 4 representatives

6 electoral votes

With six electoral votes, Nevada's voice in presidential elections is below average compared to other states.

Representing Nevada

Elected officials in Nevada represent a population with a range of interests, lifestyles, and backgrounds.

Ethnicity (2016 estimates)

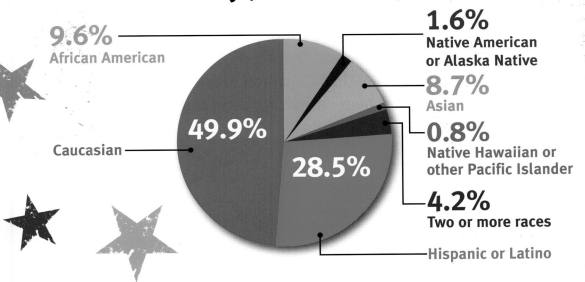

9.6%
African American

49.9%
Caucasian

28.5%

1.6%
Native American or Alaska Native

8.7%
Asian

0.8%
Native Hawaiian or other Pacific Islander

4.2%
Two or more races

Hispanic or Latino

30% speak a language other than English at home.

23% of the population have a degree beyond high school.

85% of the population graduated from high school.

94% live in cities.

55% own their own homes.

19% of Nevadans were born in other countries.

What Represents Nevada?

States choose specific animals, plants, and objects to represent the values and characteristics of the land and its people. Find out why these symbols were chosen to represent Nevada or discover surprising curiosities about them.

Seal

Nevada's state seal is packed with symbols of the state's history and landscape. They include a silver mine, mountains, and farming equipment. The state motto at the bottom of this image is "All for Our Country."

Flag

Nevada's flag has a wreath of sagebrush below a single white star. The words "Battle Born" on the banner refer to how Nevada became a state during the Civil War.

Mountain Bluebird

STATE BIRD

These beautiful birds generally sing only at dawn. The rest of the time, they are quiet.

Ichthyosaur

STATE FOSSIL

The ichthyosaur was a giant sea creature that lived more than 200 million years ago in the ocean that covered what is now Nevada.

Bristlecone Pine

STATE TREE

Bristlecone pines are among the longest living organisms in the world. Some of the ones found in Nevada are more than 4,000 years old. It was adopted as a state tree in 1987. The single-leaf piñon is another state tree adopted in 1953.

Desert Bighorn Sheep

STATE ANIMAL

Desert bighorn sheep are found around the state. Two battling desert bighorn rams, or male sheep, may crash into each other at up to 30 miles (48 km) per hour.

Sagebrush

STATE FLOWER

This tough evergreen plant is an important winter food source for the state's deer, elk, bighorn sheep, and other animals.

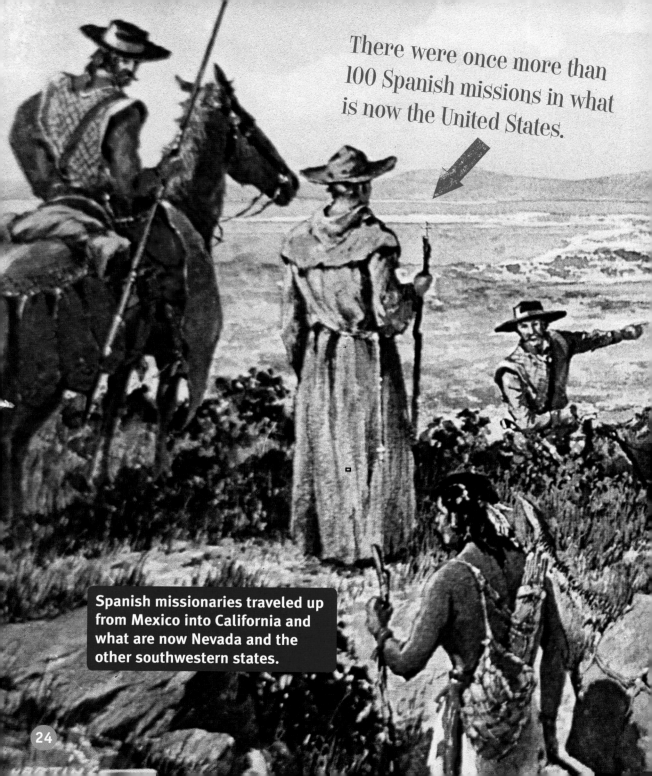

There were once more than 100 Spanish missions in what is now the United States.

Spanish missionaries traveled up from Mexico into California and what are now Nevada and the other southwestern states.

CHAPTER 3

History

It might not seem to fit the state, but the name *Nevada* comes from a Spanish word meaning "snowy." The name came from a Spanish **missionary** named Pedro Font who was traveling in California in 1776. He spotted a snow-covered mountain range to the east and named it *Sierra Nevada*, Spanish for "snowy range." As white settlers began moving into the area, they called the land Nevada, after the nearby mountains. The name stuck.

Native Americans

Pedro Font was not the first person to see the Sierra Nevada. People first arrived in what is now Nevada sometime around 9000 BCE. They likely came to hunt bison, mammoths, and other animals for food. Eventually, some of these early people started settling down in the area. They built homes and developed into four main cultures. They were the Washoe, the Northern Paiute, the Southern Paiute, and the Shoshone.

This map shows some of the major tribes that lived in what is now Nevada before Europeans came.

The Washoe used sticks and dried mud to form handmade baskets.

The Washoe lived around Lake Tahoe in summer and moved into nearby valleys for the rest of the year. They hunted animals and gathered plant foods such as nuts and berries. Northern Paiute lived to the west, where they hunted and fished. Southern Paiute lived farther south, near what is now Las Vegas. They hunted using bows and arrows. The Shoshone lived in eastern Nevada. They often used traps to catch squirrels, birds, and other small animals.

European Exploration

In 1821, Mexico claimed Nevada as part of its territory. Soon afterward, explorers from Mexico, the United States, and Europe began traveling to the area. Some people came to trap animals for their valuable furs. Others sought trails to California through the Sierra Nevada.

In 1846, the United States and Mexico went to war for control of Texas. When the United States won two years later, it took over much of Mexico's land, including Nevada.

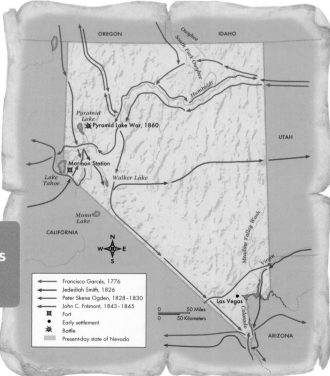

This map shows routes European explorers took as they explored and settled what is now Nevada.

In 1866, downtown Virginia City was one of Nevada's busiest areas.

During this time, many people continued to pass through Nevada on the way to California. Some people settled in Nevada to build trading posts and do business with the travelers heading west. Others built missions and tried to **convert** Native Americans to their religions. Native people mostly tolerated the new visitors at first. Clashes, however, became common as the white settlers began using up resources. Many native people also began dying from diseases they caught from settlers.

Becoming a State

Nevada changed forever in 1859, when silver was discovered. People from around the world soon flooded in, hoping to strike it rich. During this silver boom, the Civil War (1861–1865) divided the United States over the issue of **slavery**. President Abraham Lincoln wanted to add Nevada as another non-slave state to the country. This would add people and resources to his side of the war. With his support, Nevada became the 36th state in 1864.

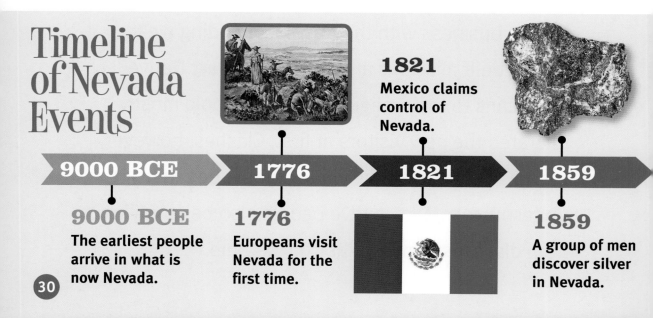

Timeline of Nevada Events

1821 Mexico claims control of Nevada.

9000 BCE → **1776** → **1821** → **1859**

9000 BCE The earliest people arrive in what is now Nevada.

1776 Europeans visit Nevada for the first time.

1859 A group of men discover silver in Nevada.

Modern Nevada

After the war, Nevada's population continued to grow. Small mining towns turned into permanent settlements. The state saw another huge growth spurt in the early 20th century. During the 1930s, thousands of people came to Nevada to work on the construction of the massive Hoover Dam. Others moved to cities such as Reno and Las Vegas to work in the casinos that opened after Nevada legalized gambling in 1931.

1905
The city of Las Vegas is founded.

1951
Scientists begin conducting tests of nuclear bombs in Nevada's deserts.

1864 **1905** **1931** **1951**

October 31, 1864
Nevada becomes the 36th state.

1931
Gambling is legalized in Nevada.

When the United States entered World War II (1939–1945) in 1941, Nevada became an important part of the war effort. Several military bases were built there, and metals mined in Nevada were used to make weapons and other supplies. After the war, the government began using Nevada's wide-open deserts to test its latest **nuclear** weapons. These tests continued until 1992. Later, studies revealed that the tests had caused cancer in people who lived nearby.

A soldier aims a machine gun during training at Las Vegas Army Airfield during World War II.

James Beckwourth

Born into slavery in Virginia, James Beckwourth grew up to have a big effect on the West. In the early 1800s, he worked as a fur trader and spent several years living with Native Americans. During this time, he became an expert in wilderness exploration. In the early 1850s, he developed the Beckwourth Trail, which began near present-day Reno, Nevada. It became a popular wagon road to California's gold country.

The International Car Forest of the Last Church is an art installation of more than 40 abandoned vehicles in the desert near Goldfield, Nevada.

CHAPTER 4

Culture

Nevada's cities and towns are lively centers of activity. Visit a museum in Reno or a historical site in Carson City. Travel to Las Vegas for a stage show or dinner at a world-class restaurant. Visit a smaller town to attend a local arts and crafts festival. If you'd rather be outside, head to Lake Tahoe to ski or snowboard. No matter where you go, you'll never run out of fun activities or amazing sights.

Fun and Games

Nevadans love the outdoors. The state's many parks and other outdoor areas are great places to hike, ride a bicycle, climb a mountain, or just camp out. Many Nevadans also play golf on the state's numerous courses.

Since 2017, Nevada's hockey fans have rooted for the Vegas Golden Knights. They also cheer for local college sports teams. Especially popular are the football and basketball teams at the University of Nevada–Las Vegas and University of Nevada–Reno.

A mountain climber rappels down a cliff above Lake Tahoe.

Held each year in Las Vegas, the National Finals Rodeo is one of the country's biggest rodeo events.

Having a Good Time

Nevada is famous for fun. People come from all over the world to let loose in Las Vegas. The state's locals, however, have plenty of their own celebrations. In Reno and other cities, you can attend annual Basque festivals. Large numbers of Basque people from Europe settled in Nevada in the 1800s. People celebrate Nevada's cowboy heritage with rodeos, where cowboys show off their riding and roping skills.

A worker tests mining samples at a Nevada gold mine.

Off to Work

More than 50 million people visit Nevada each year, making tourism the state's biggest industry. Many Nevadans in cities such as Las Vegas and Reno work at hotels, restaurants, and casinos. Another major industry is ranching. With so much wide-open space, Nevada is the perfect place to raise cattle, sheep, and other livestock. And while the silver boom ended long ago, mining is still an important part of Nevada's **economy**. The state produces copper, gold, and many useful minerals.

A Bright Future

One industry has really been heating up in Nevada in recent years: solar power. Nevada has plenty of open space and sunshine, so it is a great place for huge fields of solar panels.

In fact, experts believe it has more potential to generate solar power than any other state. As Nevada's solar industry grows, it will provide jobs and bring down energy costs in the state.

Nellis Air Force Base near Las Vegas has one of the world's largest solar power installations.

Local Cuisine

Nevada is home to countless restaurants serving creative new recipes and favorite dishes from around the world. No matter what a person likes to eat, he or she can find it in cities such as Las Vegas and Reno. Many Nevadans also enjoy dishes brought to the area by explorers, trappers, and cowboys many years ago. These include sourdough bread, beef jerky, and savory pies called pasties.

 ★ Basque Salad ★

Ask an adult to help you!

Ingredients
1 tablespoon olive oil
3 garlic cloves, crushed
3 tablespoons apple cider
   vinegar
1/2 teaspoon salt

1/2 cup mayonnaise
1 hard-boiled egg, sliced
Salad greens of any kind

Directions
Mix the oil, garlic, vinegar, salt, and mayonnaise, together in a bowl. Add the egg. Cover the bowl and set it in the refrigerator to chill. When you're ready to eat, pour your chilled dressing on your salad greens and enjoy!

What Makes Nevada Great?

With its warm weather, sunshine, beautiful views, and huge variety of things to do, Nevada is a great place to visit. Its thriving economy, diverse population, and rich culture also make it a wonderful place for people to call home. Whether you're just passing through or you've lived there your whole life, Nevada is an incredible place to be. ★

Famous People

Juanita Brooks

(1898–1989) was a historian who wrote about Mormons and the American West. She was born in Bunkerville.

Pat Nixon

(1912–1993) was First Lady of the United States during the presidency of her husband, Richard M. Nixon. She was born in Ely.

Harry Reid

(1939–) is a retired U.S. senator who represented Nevada in the U.S. Congress from 1983 to 2017. He is from Searchlight.

Jimmy Kimmel

(1967–) is a comedian who is best known as the host of the late-night talk show *Jimmy Kimmel Live!* He grew up and attended college in Las Vegas.

Andre Agassi

(1970–) is a former tennis star who is considered one of the greatest players in the game's history. He was born in Las Vegas.

Ne-Yo

(1979–) is a Grammy Award–winning singer-songwriter who has sold millions of albums. He grew up in Las Vegas.

Brandon Flowers

(1981–) is a singer-songwriter and musician. He is best known as the lead singer of the rock band The Killers. He was born in Henderson.

Gina Carano

(1982–) is an actress and martial artist who has appeared in such films as *Haywire* and *Fast and Furious 6*. She grew up in Las Vegas.

Jena Malone

(1984–) is an actress who has appeared in such films as *Pride & Prejudice* and *The Hunger Games* series. She was born in Sparks.

Colin Kaepernick

(1987–) is a professional football player who led the San Francisco 49ers to the Super Bowl in the 2012 season. Before going pro, he was a star quarterback for the University of Nevada–Reno football team.

Did You Know That ...

U.S. GOVERNMENT OWNS **85%** OF NV

About 85 percent of Nevada's land is owned by the U.S. government. This is more than any other state.

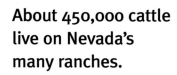

About 450,000 cattle live on Nevada's many ranches.

About half of all Nevada's counties are home to fewer than two people per square mile.

Nevada's tourists bring about $58 billion into the state's economy each year.

NV
90 times the size of
RI

As the seventh-largest state, Nevada is about 90 times the size of Rhode Island.

About 75 percent of Nevada's residents live in Clark County, the area that includes Las Vegas.

Did you find the truth?

(F) Nevada's name comes from the Spanish word for "desert."

(T) Nevada became a U.S. state during the Civil War.

Resources

Books

Nonfiction

Domnauer, Teresa. *Life in the West*. New York: Children's Press, 2010.

Heinrichs, Ann. *Nevada*. New York: Children's Press, 2014.

Fiction

Jaffe, Michele. *Bad Kitty*. New York: HarperTeen, 2006.

MacLean, Alistair. *Breakheart Pass*. New York: Doubleday, 1974.

Visit this Scholastic website for more information on Nevada:
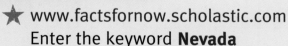 www.factsfornow.scholastic.com
Enter the keyword **Nevada**

Important Words

amendments (uh-MEND-muhnts) changes that are made to a law or a legal document

constitution (kahn-stih-TOO-shuhn) the basic laws of a country or state that detail the rights of the people and the powers of government

convert (kuhn-VURT) to convince a person to change his or her religion or other beliefs

drought (DROUT) a long period without rain; droughts damage crops and cause the soil to dry out

economy (ih-KAH-nuh-mee) the system of buying, selling, making things, and managing money in a place

missionary (MISH-uh-ner-ee) someone who is sent to a foreign country to teach about religion and do good works

nuclear (NOO-klee-ur) of or having to do with the energy created by splitting atoms

precipitation (prih-sip-i-TAY-shuhn) the falling of water from the sky in the form of rain, sleet, hail, or snow

slavery (SLAY-vur-ee) the system in which a person may be owned and thought of as property

territory (TER-ih-tor-ee) an area connected with or owned by a country that is outside the country's main borders

Index

Page numbers in **bold** indicate illustrations.

Amargosa Desert, **15**
animals, **15**, **23**, 26, 27, 28, **37**, **44**
art, **34–35**

Basque people, 37, 40
Beckwourth, James, **33**
birds, 15, **23**, 27
Boundary Peak, **7**

Carson City, **16–17**, 19
Civil War, 22, 30
climate, **13**, 14
constitution, 19

drought, **13**

early settlers, 26
economy, 38, 45
education, 18, 21
elevation, 7, **10**
explorers, 25, 28, **30**, 40

famous people, 42–43
festivals, 37
Font, Pedro, 25, 26
food, 26, 27, **40**
fur trade, 28, 33

gambling, **31**
Great Basin, **7**, 12

Hoover Dam, **7**, 31
horses, **15**
Humboldt River, 10
Humboldt Sink, 10

jobs, 31, **38**, 39

Lake Tahoe, 11, 27, 35, **36**
lakes, 7, 10, **11**, 15, 27, **36**
land, 7, **8–9**, 10, **12**, 44
languages, 21
Las Vegas, **7**, **31**, **32**, **37**, 40, 42, **45**
Lincoln, Abraham, 30
livestock, 38, **44**

maps, **6–7**, **10**, **26**, **28**
Mexico, 28, 30
military, **32**
mining, **22**, **30**, 31, 32, **38**
missionaries, **24–25**, 29
Mojave Desert, **12**
mountains, 7, 10, **11**, 12, 13, 14, 15, **22**, 25, 28, 33, **36**
music, 7, **43**

national government, 20, **42**, 44
Native Americans, 21, **26–27**, 29, 33
nuclear weapons, **31**, 32

plants, **14**, **22**, **23**, 27
population, 9, 20, 31, **45**

ranching, 38, **44**
recipe, **40**
Red Rock Canyon National Conservation Area, **8–9**
reptiles, 15
rivers, 10, 15
rodeos, **37**

sagebrush, **14**, **22**
settlers, 25, 29, 37
silver, **22**, **30**, 38
slavery, 30, 33
solar power, **39**
sports, 11, **36**, **37**, **42**, **43**
state government, **16–17**, 18, 19
statehood, 30, 31
symbols, **22–23**

timeline, **30–31**
tourism, 7, 8, 38, 45
trees, 14, **23**

Valley of Fire State Park, **12**
Virginia City, **29**

Washoe, 27
World War II, **32**

About the Author

Josh Gregory is the author of more than 120 books for kids. He has written about everything from animals to technology to history. A graduate of the University of Missouri-Columbia, he currently lives in Chicago, Illinois.